THRIVE!
An Interactive Journal
to Inspire Spiritual Growth

by
Linda Pulley Freeman

TABLE OF CONTENTS

"Your life does not get better by chance, it gets better by change." -Jim Rohn

ACKNOWLEDGMENTS

This book has been a labor of love for me, supported by the love of my family and friends. First of all, I would not have considered writing this book if it had not been for Angela, Ashanti and Richardy. Thank you for inspiring me to start writing. I would not have had the space and time to complete this book had it not been for the support of my husband, David, my children, Zachary, Daniella and Vanessa, my niece, Nina and my Mom, Anne. Thank you for loving me. I would not have had the confidence to finish the book had it not been for my friends who read the early manuscript and provided me with their feedback. Thank you for your enthusiasm. I would not have experienced such a smooth editing process had it not been for my friend, Professor Julie Exposito. I would not have had such a cool cover design had it not been for my friend and creative genius Johanne Wilson, co-founder of Cool Creative, Inc. Thank you for sharing your creativity with me and bringing the sunflower to life. Finally, thank you to my ministry mentors: Wanda Burgund and Pastors Rich and Robyn Wilkerson, who opened the door to my second career.

INTRODUCTION

"The greatest thing is, at any moment, to be willing to give up who we are in order to become all that we can become."
- Max De Pree

I began writing this book as a journal for myself.

Recent events in my life had left me feeling weighed down by a load I could not lift. I had never experienced sadness so profound. Because of this, I began to compile Bible stories, scriptures and quotes by famous people into categories like peace, courage and faith – just to encourage myself. I would research and compile Scripture daily, adding to it my thoughts and my prayers. I knew that in order for me to come out of my sadness and move forward, I needed a new perspective. I needed to strengthen myself. The past was never coming back and the future was not waiting for me. I have been keeping a journal since I was in junior high school in the mid-70s. I have a file cabinet full of journals in my office and those are only the ones dating back to the early 90's. My journals are the chronicles of my life, both the ups and the downs. Until that time I had also used my journals as a planner, keeping track of my goals and aspirations. However, at a certain point the future suddenly seemed like a vast, open space; a gaping nothingness. As I continued to compile and write, I began to ask myself some questions like:

- What have I accomplished?
- Did it matter?
- Who am I and who do I want to be?
- What am I going to do next?
- What do I want?
- What does God want from me?

I could not answer. I kept writing. The journal grew and I began to feel my load lifting. I realized that I was crafting a roadmap for the next phase of my life. Some months later, two young women asked me if I would mentor them. They were feeling like they were at a crossroads and wanted someone to help them walk through it. Surprisingly (or maybe not so surprisingly), they were asking me the questions I had been asking myself. They had no idea that I had been researching, writing and praying about those same things for months and months. I had heard so often that your "test becomes your testimony" and been inspired many times by the testimony of others who had victoriously come through tremendous trials. However, my honest thought was always, "That's an amazing testimony, but I am happy without one, Lord!" Notwithstanding, here I was mentoring these young women, using the journal entries I had written to encourage myself. I never would have written any of it had it not been for my own tough time of searching.

This book represents my journey of self-discovery and personal strategic planning as well as what I have been learning and sharing. I have titled it THRIVE! This word invokes a spirit of motivation, inspiration, growth and excitement in me. According to Dictionary.com, the word thrive means "to prosper, to be fortunate, to be successful, to flourish". I chose the sunflower for the cover image because the sunflower represents vibrancy and enthusiasm to me. As I was writing I wanted all of those things. I wanted to be vibrant, motivated, inspired and successful. I wanted to THRIVE! This book was intentionally designed to be a 40-day, interactive journal. The number 40 represents a period of testing or trial in the Bible. This testing is often followed by a renewed sense of purpose and intensity. For instance, the Israelites spent 40 years in the desert, but emerged to enter their Promised Land (Deuteronomy 8:2-5). Elijah traveled for 40 days and nights to reach Mt. Horeb (I Kings 19:8), but emerged to hear the voice of God directing him to his next mission. Jesus spent 40 days in the desert being tested by Satan, but emerged to begin his three-year ministry (Matthew 4:2).

In addition to the Biblical significance of the number 40, many studies have been conducted on how long it takes to break a habit and form a new one. The total number of days ranges anywhere from 21 to 46 days. (If you are interested in more information on habits, refer to Charles Duhigg's book, "The Power of Habit".) Over the course of this 40-day study, I believe that you will have time to clarify: who you are on a deeper level, what is important to you and where you want to focus your energy. You can also kick start changing habits that don't serve you well. I have created a Thrive Journal Kit at thethrivejournal.org where you can find additional materials and tools you can use as you work through this book. You can also interact with me and other readers on this website. As you apply yourself, you will emerge from this 40-day experience with renewed purpose and intensity. You will be encouraged and inspired, as I have been. Get ready to THRIVE!

Be blessed,

Linda

"First say to yourself what you would be and then do what you have to do." —Epictetus

"For I will pour out water to quench your thirst and to irrigate your parched fields. And I will pour out my Spirit on your descendants, and my blessing on your children. They will thrive like watered grass, like willows on a riverbank." Isaiah 44:3-4

Advice from a Tree

Stand tall and proud

Sink your roots

Into the earth

Be content with

Your natural beauty

Go out on a limb

Drink plenty of water

Enjoy the view

-Unknown

PART ONE: DISCOVERING

"The world is full of people who will go their whole lives and not actually live one day. She did not intend on being one of them." -Unknown

"You saw me before I was born. Every day of my life was recorded in your book. Every moment was laid out before a single day had passed." Psalm 139:16

DAY 1
BEGINNINGS

Today's Date:

Read Psalm 139:13-18

Our lives have a start date and an end date. We never know when either date will occur. Only God knows, but from the minute we are born, the clock is ticking. Not only that, we were born with an unspecified set of skills, abilities, talents and family/community conditions. We are not given an itinerary or an inventory, but what we are given is the opportunity to live. We have the opportunity to utilize those skills, abilities and talents to build our lives. It is this opportunity that is described in Hebrews 12:1, "And let us run with endurance the race God has set before us." Taking time to focus on yourself, understanding who you are and creating a blueprint for your life requires effort. It also requires that you understand how valuable you are and how purpose-full your life is. Lastly, it requires a personal commitment that you are going to make the most of the resources and the talents God has given you. Taking the time to step back and recognize them says, "I matter" and not just to yourself, but also to your family, to your community and to the world at large. There is something inside of you waiting to unfold. There is no better time than now to discover what that is.

I have had the privilege of attending and teaching many leadership classes. The topic of personal leadership, or leading your own life, is typically the first on the syllabus in a leadership class. Who am I? Why am I here? How do I lead my own life and am I leading myself in the right direction? These are important questions that only you can answer. Answering these questions is the focal point of Part I. During the first 16 days you will establish your core values, vision and mission. Plan to spend about an hour per day setting up this important foundation. So much of life in our culture is focused on externals: how we look, what we wear, what our profession is, what we own and who we know. However, the Scripture tells us: "So we fix our eyes not on what is seen, but on what is unseen, since what is seen is temporary, but what is unseen is eternal" (2 Corinthians 4:18; NIV). In the pursuit of the externals, we may neglect our inner life which is unseen. King David, who obtained all the externals, wrote these lines in Psalm 139:1, 23-24, "O Lord, you have examined my heart and know everything about me... Search me, O God, and know my heart; test me and know my anxious thoughts. Point out anything in me that offends you, and lead me along the path of everlasting life."

David was on a journey of self-discovery, of under-standing who he was in relation to God. He wasn't crying out to God for more material success. I encourage you, as you work through Part I, to give yourself time to explore who you are. Be honest with yourself. Be like David and ask God to examine your heart. Be ready for change. Be open to new ideas. Emerge from the first 16 days of this study having discovered the "seed" of who you are. That seed is yours to protect. That seed is yours to grow. That seed is yours to nurture until it thrives. Part II is a 28-day devotional journal, created to help you establish a daily routine of prayer, meditation, reflection, exercise and alignment with what you developed in Part I. This is the process that I have been working through in my morning routine for years. Every morning, I get up, brush my teeth and then sit down on my yoga mat. I read a passage of scripture, meditate on it, write down some thoughts about it, review the coming day, pray and finally, I spend some time exercising. Oh yes, then I enjoy a cup of coffee. The amount of time I spend in my morning routine varies, but I make it my habit to place myself on that mat every morning.

Some days I wake up energized, ready to go, looking forward to the day. Some days I wake up, remember what's on my calendar and sigh. On those days, I have to push myself to go to the mat and stick to the routine. In either case, the routine is a comfort and an encouragement. Not to mention, daily scripture reading, prayer, meditation and exercise yield great results.

"Find the seed at the bottom of your heart and bring forth a flower." -Shigenori Kameoka

DAY 1 NOTES

Each day you will have the opportunity to write out some thoughts, plans, challenges, prayers and a note of gratitude. Over the course of the next 40 days, you will be able to appreciate the changes, answers and opportunities that will have opened up for you.

Thoughts for today

Plans for today

Challenges for today

Prayer for today

Today, I am grateful for

[Note: Please begin to gather copies of your favorite magazines and a glue stick. We will use this in Chapter 4.]

"Don't waste your time living someone else's life."

-*Chris Guillebeau*

"The Lord says, 'I will guide you along the best pathway for your life. I will advise you and watch over you.'"
Psalm 32:8

DAY 2
BEGINNINGS, PART TWO

Today's Date:

Read Jeremiah 29:11-13

Today's activity involves taking a personal inventory. This inventory will be your starting point. Answer these questions on a separate sheet of paper or download today's worksheet.

- When do you feel the happiest?
- What would you say have been your greatest accomplishments?
- What are the greatest challenges that you have overcome?

- What's great about you?
- What would you like to improve upon?
- What do you enjoy most about life?
- What are some things you have yet to accomplish?
- If money were no object, what would you do?
- Is there a dream in your heart that you have suppressed?

Is there a habit you need to end, or one you need to begin? Take your time thinking about these questions throughout the day. Over the next few days, you will be able to weave these answers into the next days' activities.

"Do not despise these small beginnings, for the Lord rejoices to see the work begin..." Zechariah 4:10

DAY 2 NOTES

Thoughts for today

Plans for today

Challenges for today

Prayer for today

Today, I am grateful for

"When inspiration does not come to me, I go halfway to meet it." -Sigmund Freud

"Jesus Christ is the same yesterday, today, and forever. So do not be attracted by strange, new ideas. Your strength comes from God's grace..." Hebrews 13:8, 9

DAY 3
BUILDING A FOUNDATION

Today's Date:

Read Hebrews 13:1-9

Our core values form a foundation from which we conduct ourselves and develop our lifestyles. We cling to our core values even in the face of danger and uncertainty. You may have core values that you have never articulated, but they still govern your daily decisions and clarify who you are to those around you. One of my family's core values is education. We value education. We have made many sacrifices to ensure that our children have received a quality education, including music lessons and many other extra-curricular activities. We were clear and convinced about why those sacrifices were important. Owning your core values will help you to make major life decisions with confidence. If an opportunity or a decision is in conflict with one of your core values, you must say no. Of course, if an opportunity or a decision is aligned with one of your core values, you must consider saying yes. In the Thrive Journal Kit on the website, you can download the worksheet for Day 3 with foundation bricks and a list of common values. If you don't see a value that you hold, fill out a blank foundation brick. Use a glue stick to paste them to your life foundation below.

"It's not enough to have lived. We should be determined to live for something." -Winston Churchill

MY LIFE FOUNDATION

"Not everything that can be counted counts and not everything that counts can be counted." -Albert Einstein

DAY 3 NOTES

Thoughts for today

Plans for today

Challenges for today

Prayer for today

Today, I am grateful for

"All that is gold does not glitter, not all those who wander are lost; the old that is strong does not wither, deep roots are not reached by the frost." -J.R.R. Tolkien

"Then the angel showed me a river with the water of life, clear as crystal, flowing from the throne of God and of the Lamb. It flowed down the center of the main street. On each side of the river grew a tree of life, bearing twelve crops of fruit, with a fresh crop each month. The leaves were used for medicine to heal the nations." Revelation 22:1-2

DAY 4
WHAT DO YOU SEE?

Today's Date:

Read Revelation 22:1-5

*I*n today's reading, the Apostle John was recounting a vision he had been shown of the future. This vision was awesome, inspiring, and encouraging. Creating a vision of your future can be as powerful. Who are you? Who will you become? Where will you be? Who and what will surround you?

Can you see it? To help answer these questions, I want you to create a vision collage. A vision collage is a collection of pictures that represents you: who you are and who you want to become. What I would like you to do for this exercise is to first open a Pinterest account, if you don't already have one. Go to www.pinterest.com for information on how to join and create your own account. I have been developing a Vision Board on Pinterest while I was writing this book. You can find my Pinterest boards at pinterest.com/linda462009. If you follow me, I will follow you back and we can interact about our ideas there! Pinterest allows you to "pin" photos to a virtual board. You can use your own photos or you can "re-pin" photos from anyone on Pinterest onto your board(s).

If you would rather not open a Pinterest account, you will need some magazines, a glue stick, and a pair of scissors. If you see anything on Pinterest or in the magazines that represents the life you want to lead, such as a place you want to live, your favorite colors, clothes you really like, a piece of furniture, food you enjoy, words that resonate with you or anything else that catches your eye, cut it out or "re-pin" in Pinterest. If you have cut out pictures, arrange the pictures you have cut out on the following pages and attached with the glue stick. Work on this for a while and then walk away. When you come back, take a look. Do these pictures help you create a mental picture of what a **thriving** life looks like for you? Maybe you need to keep looking for pictures. Take your time; this is really important. In fact, don't feel like you need to complete your collage today. Open your eyes, open your mind and open your heart. Keep working at it. I am still adding pictures to my Pinterest boards. I am enjoying it!

"I dream of painting and then I paint my dream."
-Vincent Van Gogh

DAY 4 NOTES

Thoughts for today

Plans for today

Challenges for today

Prayer for today

Today, I am grateful for

"Don't let someone else's opinion of you become your reality." -Les Brown

"You must find that place inside yourself where nothing is impossible." -Deepak Chopra

VISION COLLAGE

"The past cannot be changed. The future is yet in your power." -Mary Pickford

"Live out of your imagination, not your history."
-Stephen Covey

VISION COLLAGE

"Don't go with the flow. You are the flow." *-Sugi Tanaka*

"Then the LORD said to me, 'Write my answer plainly on tablets, so that a runner may carry the correct message to others. This vision is for a future time. It describes the end, and it will be fulfilled. If it seems slow in coming, wait patiently, for it will surely take place. It will not be delayed.'" Habakkuk 2:2-3

DAY 5
SPEAKING YOUR VISION

Today's Date:

Read Habakkuk 2:2-3

*L*ook at your Vision Collage. How is it coming along? How would you describe who you want to become, using those pictures, in eight to ten sentences? The more clarity you can give to your vision, the better. Your vision needs to be clear. Don't worry about the exact time when the vision will come together.

Write your sentences here:

_____

_____

_____

_____

_____

_____

_____

"Life isn't about finding yourself. Life is about creating yourself." -George Bernard Shaw

DAY 5 NOTES

Thoughts for today

Plans for today

Challenges for today

Prayer for today

Today, I am grateful for

"Success in any endeavor depends on the degree to which it is an expression of your true self." -Ralph Marston

"But Moses protested again, "What if they won't believe me or listen to me? What if they say, "The Lord never appeared to you'?" Exodus 4:1

DAY 6
SPEAKING YOUR VISION, PART TWO

🙰

Today's Date:

Read Exodus 4:1-17

Moses was having an identity crisis. From childhood, he believed that he was an Egyptian prince. Unexpectedly, he found out that he was descended from a Hebrew slave. In today's reading, he was not living as either a prince or a slave; he was living with nomads in the desert. Moses was hiding from who he was. However, when God spoke to Moses, God was confident about who He was, who Moses was and who Moses was destined to be. Knowing who you are and who you are to become brings confidence and resolve. Today, revisit your vision collage. Condense the vision sentences that you wrote yesterday down to one or two. Be convinced about who you are and who you want to become. Say it out loud. Revise it until it truly represents you. Tell it to a friend. Write it on this page. Write it on a "Speak It Out" note page in your Thrive Journal Kit and tape it to your bathroom mirror or your refrigerator. Write it below:

_____

_____

_____

_____

_____

"The idea is to write it so that people hear it and it slides through the brain and goes straight to the heart."
-Maya Angelou

DAY 6 NOTES

Thoughts for today

Plans for today

Challenges for today

Prayer for today

Today, I am grateful for

"Your spark can become a flame and change everything."

-E.D. Nixon

"When I heard this, I sat down and wept. In fact, for days I mourned, fasted and prayed to the God of heaven."

Nehemiah 1:4

DAY 7
BIG IDEAS

Today's Date:

Read Nehemiah 1:1-11

N ehemiah had a big idea. After hearing the stories about the condition of the people living in Jerusalem, he decided that he wanted to rebuild that broken down city. Your ideas might have come to you as a picture in your mind's eye or a sentence floating through your thoughts. They might have come to you in your dreams while you slept. They may have come as a vision while you were awake, involved in a totally unrelated activity. Nehemiah's idea came to him after many days of prayer and fasting about something that troubled him; the conditions in Jerusalem. He wanted to be part of the solution. It was a big idea.

Are any of your ideas so big that you can't even imagine how they will ever be accomplished? Are you looking at your vision collage and wondering, "How is that ever going to happen?" Are you thinking, "I am too young or too old for a big idea?" If you have any of these thoughts, you are in good company. Nehemiah's idea was big for many reasons. One, Nehemiah was a cupbearer. His job was to ensure that none of the king's drinks were poisoned. He was neither an architect nor an urban planner. Two, he was not a wealthy businessman with millions of dollars to invest in economic development. He knew nothing about the business of building a city. Another challenge was that the people that lived in the surrounding communities would not benefit from a strong, vibrant Jerusalem. They would resist any effort to rebuild it. However, Nehemiah's big idea was aligned with God's plans. As Nehemiah fasted and prayed, the big idea began to take shape in his mind.

God's word tells us in Joel 2:28-29: "Then, after doing all those things, I will pour out my Spirit upon all people. Your sons and daughters will prophesy. Your old men will dream dreams, and your young men will see visions. In those days I will pour out my Spirit even on servants – men and women alike." Know that God is pouring out His Spirit. He is pouring it out on the young and the old, men and women. He is filling them with dreams and visions; new big ideas from His plans. Be open to receive a big idea from God.

"To have a great idea, have a lot of them."
-Thomas Edison

"An idea that is not dangerous is unworthy of being called an idea at all." -Oscar Wilde

DAY 7 NOTES

Thoughts for today

Plans for today

Challenges for today

Prayer for today

Today, I am grateful for

"I replied, 'If it please the king, and if you are pleased with me, your servant, send me to Judah to rebuild the city where my ancestors are buried.'" Nehemiah 2:5

DAY 8
YOUR BIG IDEAS

Today's Date:

Read Nehemiah 2:1-8

Nehemiah went through five distinct stages to set his big idea in motion:

- He heard. When Nehemiah heard about the condition of Jerusalem and its people, he was devastated. He recognized that there was a need and he knew that something had to be done, but he did not know what.

- He prayed. Nehemiah took the time to ask God what could be done about the problem. He knew that the solution would need God's assistance.

- He conceived. As he was praying and fasting, he conceived an idea in his mind.

- He spoke. Nehemiah waited until just the right moment to speak his idea out loud. When he spoke, he was ready to discuss details.

- He worked. Nehemiah immersed himself in transforming his idea into reality through hard work.

Follow his example to nurture your own big idea. Take the time to fast and pray, like Nehemiah did. Be patient. Wait for an idea to form. Be prudent about discussing your ideas with others. Notice that when Nehemiah spoke, he spoke to someone who did not see the idea as impossible. The king thought about big ideas all the time; not only that, the king was able to provide some invaluable input and resources. Finally, Nehemiah worked. Work is the fuel that will bring your big idea to life.

"A man may die, nations may rise and fall, but an idea lives on." -John F. Kennedy

DAY 8 NOTES

Thoughts for today

Plans for today

Challenges for today

Prayer for today

Today, I am grateful for

"What would you attempt to do if you knew you could not fail?" —Unknown

"But you will receive power when the Holy Spirit comes on you. And you will be my witnesses, telling people about me everywhere – in Jerusalem, throughout Judea, in Samaria, and to the ends of the earth." Acts 1:8

DAY 9
MISSION CRITICAL

Today's Date:

Read Acts 1:1-11

*I*f someone were to ask you, "What were you born to do?" you should be able to give him or her an answer. Your mission statement is not a reflection of who you are or who you will become. Rather, your mission statement is a description of what you were born to do. In her book *The Path* Laurie Beth Jones suggests that your mission statement should be short and concise, easy to memorize and share. Your mission statement should complement the concept of who you will become (your vision), as well as your core values. In Acts 1:8, we can read the very short, concise mission statement that the disciples received from Jesus. The remaining books of the New Testament give us a clear picture of what they did to carry out their mission.

There may be some things that you do now that have no relationship to your core values and vision. It can happen if you are not confident, or it can happen if you are focused on what other people think. Either way, expect internal conflict when what you do does not reflect what you believe is important. Frustration, boredom, disappointment, depression and regret can begin to creep in. For people on a timeline with an unspecified end date, not having a defined mission is really a tragedy. Start developing your mission statement by reviewing your vision statement. What action verbs would best describe your vision if it was alive and happening? Examples of strong action verbs include words such as run, lead, write, build and explore. In your Thrive Journal Kit, download the worksheet for Day 9. There is a set of verbs for you to consider with some blanks to write down additional verbs that are meaningful to you. Use your glue sticks and glue the verbs that you feel most closely connects to your vision below:

"You really can change the world if you care enough."

-Marian Wright Edelman

"I'm thankful to those who said **no***; because of them I did it myself." -Albert Einstein*

DAY 9 NOTES

Thoughts for today

Plans for today

Challenges for today

Prayer for today

Today, I am grateful for

"There is no substitute for hard work."
-Thomas Edison

"The members of the council were amazed when they saw the boldness of Peter and John, for they could see that they were ordinary men with no special training in the Scriptures. They also recognized them as men who had been with Jesus." Acts 4:13

DAY 10
MISSION CRITICAL, PART TWO

Today's Date:

Read Acts 4:1-20

In the business world, if the success of an entire operation hinges on the viability of a person or thing, that person or that thing is considered "mission critical". Peter and John understood that preaching the Gospel was mission critical to the purpose of their lives. They were willing to endure any hardship to ensure that the mission was accomplished. Your mission statement should represent the actions that are mission critical for you to fulfill the purpose for which you were born. Developing your mission statement will take time, so do not hesitate to put this book down for a while and think about it. Get out some sheets of paper and keep drafting. Use the action verbs that you selected yesterday. Once you have it worked out, write it below. Don't forget to also write it on a "Speak it Out" note and post it up on your bathroom mirror, next to your vision.

MY MISSION CRITICAL:

_____

_____

_____

_____

_____

DAY 10 NOTES

Thoughts for today

Plans for today

Challenges for today

Prayer for today

Today, I am grateful for

"We are the ones we have been waiting for."
-Hopi teaching

"Have the people of Israel build me a holy sanctuary so I can live among them... Be sure that you make everything according to the pattern I have shown you here on the mountain." Exodus 25:8, 40

DAY 11
GOAL-SETTING FOR SUCCESS

Today's Date:

Read Exodus 25

The thread that connects your mission to your daily life is woven into your schedule by way of your goals. God gave the people of Israel the goal of building a sanctuary, according to His specific plans. God's plans were very detailed. The most effective goals are well defined with an estimate of how long it will take to accomplish and what resources you will need. Early in my marriage, I convinced my husband to buy into a parenting goal that included having two children and spacing them out in such a way that they would both graduate from college by the time we reached age 50. Twenty-seven years later, our second child would graduate from college with her bachelor's degree, right between my 50th birthday and my husband's 50th birthday in May 2013. Following the plan, our first child graduated from college a few years earlier. Whew! We worked that out!

Sometimes the process of goal-setting can result in an enormous "To Do" list. Short-term, intermediate and long-term goals can multiply exponentially, especially in an organization. Often people become so overwhelmed by all the lists that they just shut down. Their eyes glaze over. Sometimes those goals mysteriously disappear into a big, 3-ring binder, never to be seen again. That's not what I am suggesting that you do here. I am suggesting that you keep it simple. Dr. James Davis, founder of the World Leaders' Conference, teaches that no more than six goals should be developed. He compared goals to the balls a juggler juggles. Very few jugglers can juggle more than six balls at the same time with precision. In this case, let's consider ourselves as jugglers.

> *"Discipline is the refining fire by which talent becomes ability." -Roy L. Smith*

Your Goals

What goals, if accomplished, would assist you in completing your mission? You might want to make a list of the ideas you have on a separate piece of paper first. Possibly, some of them could be grouped together. Select a maximum of six.

Goal #1: _____

Goal #2: _____

Goal #3: _____

Goal #4: _____

Goal #5: _____

Goal #6: _____

"Doing more things faster is no substitute for doing the right things." -Stephen Covey

DAY 11 NOTES

Thoughts for today

Plans for today

Challenges for today

Prayer for today

Today, I am grateful for

"...And the king granted these requests, because the gracious hand of God was on me. When I came to the governors of the province west of the Euphrates River, I delivered the king's letters to them. The king, I should add, had sent along army officers and horsemen to protect me." Nehemiah 2:8b-9

DAY 12
RESOURCES

Today's Date:

Read Nehemiah 2

*B*ig ideas need big resources. Nehemiah possessed none of the resources he needed to rebuild the walls around Jerusalem. He had no money, workers, tools, wood, bricks, or even transportation to Jerusalem. However, he had a relationship with the King and that turned out to be his greatest resource. In your case, what are the resources you need to achieve your goals? For each one of your goals, write out the resources that you think you need. Are there people you know who might be able to serve as a resource? Is there any additional education or experience you may need to obtain?

Download the worksheet for Day 12 or complete the chart below.

Goal #1: _____

Resource List

Goal #2: _____

Resource List

Goal #3: _____

Resource List

Goal #4: _____

Resource List

Goal #5: _____

Resource List

Goal #6: _____

Resource List

"Even strong young lions sometimes go hungry, but those who trust in the Lord will lack no good thing."
Psalm 34:10

"Small opportunities are often the beginnings of great enterprises." -Demosthenes

DAY 12 NOTES

Thoughts for today

Plans for today

Challenges for today

Prayer for today

Today, I am grateful for

"If you only have a hammer, you tend to see every problem as a nail." -Abraham Maslow

"Then the Lord asked him, 'What is that in your hand?' 'A shepherd's staff,' Moses replied."

Exodus 4:2

DAY 13
WHAT DO YOU HAVE?

Today's Date:

Read Exodus 4:1-17

Are there items on your resource lists that you already have access to or can easily have access to? Does your list include items that require other people to get involved or additional education or certification(s) that you need to obtain? Try to make some detailed notes on your resource lists that describe what you need to do next to obtain those items. Don't allow yourself to become discouraged in the details. Be encouraged that you are bringing clarity to your goals. When Moses heard what God planned for him to do, he was discouraged.

He believed he was the wrong person for the job. In many ways, he appeared to be less prepared than Nehemiah was to rebuild the walls of Jerusalem. Moses was a fugitive, hiding from the Egyptian authorities. He had no intention of ever returning to Egypt, much less going into Pharaoh's palace with a demand. He didn't even have the proper attire or grooming to be acknowledged as a worthy palace guest. He had just spent the last 40 years of his life as a shepherd in the desert.

However, here is an important principle that we can draw from today's reading: if God is your partner, you have everything you need! Moses had very real concerns about returning to Egypt. Plus, he didn't know if anyone in his family was still alive, yet God encouraged him to go back to Egypt. God would provide the proper resources, at the right time, if Moses would get going. You may have very real concerns about your capacity and your resources, too. Be encouraged by Moses's story. Get going!

> *"It is never too late! Start where you are. Use what you have. Do what you can." -Arthur Ashe*

DAY 13 NOTES

Thoughts for today

Plans for today

Challenges for today

Prayer for today

Today, I am grateful for

"We are not creatures of circumstance; we are creators of circumstance." -Benjamin Disraeli

"Noah did everything exactly as God had commanded him." Genesis 6:22

DAY 14
THE CLASH

🙢

Today's Date:

Read Genesis 6:9-22

F or the last thirteen days, you have been contemplating and writing about your mission, vision, values. You have been working on your vision collage. You have also spent time developing your goals. I hope that you have uncovered some thoughts and ideas that have energized you. Take that energy and use it for this next step: integrating into your daily life all of the plans you have written. This is where your ideas will be transformed from the theoretical to the practical. This is also where you will encounter The Clash. The Clash arises when you discover realities in your everyday life that are contrary or worlds away from your new plans. The Clash can be with a personal routine, a habit, or a relationship. You are going to have to draw on that newfound energy and inspiration and **push** through The Clash.

There are 28 days remaining in this study. According to the research, before you finish this book you have the time to make some changes that you will be able to maintain. You can form a new habit before you finish the last page of this book. When God told Noah His plan to destroy the earth with a flood, Noah was faced with The Clash. God told him that everything in his life and world was about to change. Noah had a choice: 1) agree and participate or 2) remain the same. God did not tell him when the flood was coming. There probably wasn't a cloud in the sky. He only gave him the directions for building the ark. This account tells us that Noah changed his daily routine into an ark-building routine. It could not have been easy, yet he chose to change and follow the new plan God had given him. He chose to live.

In our case, we most likely will never face a catastrophic event like the flood Noah was expecting. Consequently, we may never be as motivated as Noah to adjust our routines. However, in order to achieve the goals we have written down, we must change how we view our daily routines and be willing to make changes. Some of those changes will be tough. Let's start by writing out your most typical morning, using the template below.

One "Day by Hour" Typical Morning Planning Template

6am _____

7am _____

8am _____

9am _____

10am _____

11am _____

12pm _____

"All our life, so far as it has definite form, is but a mass of habits." -William James

When you look at your typical morning, how do your morning activities relate to your goals? Can you visualize a pathway leading from your morning activities to the completion of some or any of your goals? Possibly, there are activities on your schedule that you cannot immediately adjust, like a work schedule or a school schedule. Maybe you need to slightly revise your goals or your morning schedule. Maybe you have just encountered The Clash. My advice is to start with small changes. Small changes can be significant changes. Now, you can use the following Typical Afternoon Planning Template to create your afternoon schedule. Is there a change that you can make today?

One "Day by Hour" Typical Afternoon Planning Template

1pm _____

2pm _____

3pm _____

4pm _____

5pm _____

6pm _____

7pm _____

"We do what we are and we are what we do."

-Abraham Maslow

DAY 14 NOTES

Thoughts for today

Plans for today

Challenges for today

Prayer for today

Today, I am grateful for

"Hold fast to dreams for if dreams die, life is a broken winged bird that cannot fly." -Langston Hughes

"Take care of your body. It's the only place you have to live." -Jim Rohn

DAY 15
DON'T FORGET TO EXERCISE

Today's Date:

Read 1 Corinthians 9:24-27

One thing about creating a strategic plan for your life is that you need to be alive to carry it out. True, we don't know the length of our lives, but we can impact the quality of our lives by taking care of our health. How have you included your health in your plans so far? Did you make time in your schedule for exercise? What about your eating habits? Many people have asked me, "How can I incorporate exercise into my life?" They give me many reasons why they have never been able to get started. Their reasons are all valid for the lives they are leading, including their work schedules, their children's schedules, their general dislike of anything resembling exercise and their general health status (high blood pressure, obesity, or joint problems). The answer I give to everyone is: "Just begin." If you don't exercise at all or just occasionally, begin with baby steps. Observe your weekly schedule. How many hours do you spend sleeping, working, watching TV, or doing other activities?

Is there something you can cut back on or adjust so that you can make space to take care of your body? I am sure that the answer is **yes**. You can carve out a 30 minute space every day to walk around the block. Every day, use those thirty minutes to move your body in the exercise of your choice. Just begin. Also, think about your eating habits. What you eat is the fuel that enables your body to keep moving. Is there something in your regular diet that you know isn't good for you, like soda, candy, fried food, fast food? Pick just one thing and stop eating it. Just begin to make a change. I promise you that once you begin, you will start to feel better and look better. The improvements will inspire you to keep going.

Whatever type of exercise program you decide to try, begin slowly and build an exercise routine into your daily life that is enjoyable and sustainable. I guarantee that if you pick an exercise style that you do not enjoy, making it a daily habit will be nearly impossible. For now, if starting with a 30 minute walk around your neighborhood is enjoyable and fits into your schedule, do that! The most important thing in beginning an exercise program is the self-awareness that your body is a precious commodity worthy of your care and attention. Just begin. Make it a part of your daily schedule.

> *"The secret of getting ahead is getting started."*
> *-Sally Berger*

DAY 15 NOTES

Thoughts for today

Plans for today

Challenges for today

Prayer for today

Today, I am grateful for

"Everyone thinks of changing the world, but no one thinks of changing himself." -Leo Tolstoy

"In the beginning God created the heavens and the earth. The earth was formless and empty, and darkness covered the deep waters. And the Spirit of God was hovering over the surface of the waters." Genesis 1:1- 2

DAY 16
WITH INTENTION

Today's Date:

Read Genesis 1:1-31

Today you can look back and see what you have accomplished so far in this study. You have created a blueprint, a design with your unique style. This blueprint is on paper or on Pinterest. This blueprint represents you in two dimensions. The challenge today is to set your intention to make that blueprint come to life in multiple dimensions. Only you can do this. When the Spirit of God hovered over the waters, His blueprint for creation was not yet multi-dimensional. It existed in the

Spirit. When God spoke, the elements began to move in ways that we cannot fully understand. Creation took shape, form and function by the Word of God. It became animated, living, growing and moving. In a similar way, you must have faith to believe that as you begin to speak, elements in your life will begin to shift. As you follow your new daily schedule, patterns will be broken and new ones will form. Your unique plan will also become animated, living, growing and moving.

One person who has a history of setting his intention is my son, Zachary. When he was 12, he announced that he was going to be a guitar player and that he would play football in college. At the time, he did not own a guitar. He had never played football on a team. However, he insisted that all he needed was a guitar and to get on a football team. We bought a guitar and signed him up for guitar lessons. In ninth grade he started playing high school football. He never wavered, but he would continuously remind us of his goals and what resources he needed from us. He would talk to us for hours about guitars and amps, struts and strings, cleats and gloves, protein shakes and weight-training.

Zachary is now 23 years old. He is a guitarist and vocalist, as well as one of the worship leaders at our church. He has co-written and performed songs that you can download from iTunes. He graduated from Cornell College playing defensive tackle on its football team for four years. How did that happen? Zachary repeatedly talked about what he was going to accomplish. He stayed focused, practicing for hours on the guitar. He only missed two football practices in four years of high school. He even hobbled on crutches to football practice after a knee surgery in college. He was relentless. I have learned so much from Zachary and how to achieve goals. The three words that come to mind when I think of Zachary are intention, focus and persistence. Apply those three words to your own life. Make up your mind that your plans are good, that the outcomes will be good and that you are good. Don't wait for somebody else to validate your plan: set your intention! Focus! Be persistent!

"The real moment of success is not the moment apparent to the crowd." -George Bernard Shaw

DAY 16 NOTES

Thoughts for today

Plans for today

Challenges for today

Prayer for today

Today, I am grateful for

"Act and God will act." -Joan of Arc

PART TWO:
NURTURING

"The purpose of life is a life of purpose."
-Robert Byrne

"You don't have enough faith," Jesus told them. "I tell you the truth, if you had faith even as small as a mustard seed, you could say to this mountain, 'Move from here to there,' and it would move. Nothing would be impossible." Matthew 17:20

DAY 17
FAITH

Today's Date:

Read Matthew 17:14-20

*F*aith is potent. Have you ever held a mustard seed in your hand? A mustard seed is approximately 1/20th of an inch in size. That's small. However, Jesus told the disciples that if they had faith as small as a mustard seed, nothing would be impossible for them. **Nothing.** They could cast a demon out of a boy just as easily as move an entire mountain to a new location. However, like the disciples, I have been guilty many times of not having enough faith. I have also been guilty in thinking that the little bit of faith that I had at the time was not enough for the situation I was facing. What about you? Have there been situations in your life that have made you feel that you did not have enough faith or you questioned the little faith you had? If so, we are in good company with the disciples. At times faith was a struggle for them, too.

In my case, my struggles with faith are rooted in my tendency to put my faith in my own abilities. Then, when I am confronted with a situation that I feel is beyond my ability to handle, I am shaken. My mind begins to race with all the possibilities of trouble and doom. I think about that problem day and night. I let it grow and grow in my mind, until my faith is dwarfed by my fear of the situation. When Jesus said, "Have faith in God" to the disciples, He was talking to us as well. Here's the thought that I have been meditating on: that mustard seed faith is not a feeling, nor is it situational, but rather it is a conviction. Mustard seed faith is the conviction that God is exactly everything He has revealed to us. He knows us. He knows our situations. He loves us and He has the power to overcome any and all circumstances. Mustard seed faith is focused on God and then energized by God. If we have faith in God even as small as a mustard seed, as Jesus said, the energy to change a seemingly impossible problem will flow from God through us. The mountain will move.

> *"Don't let your hearts be troubled. Trust in God, and trust also in me." John 14:1*

DAY 17 NOTES

Thoughts for today

Plans for today

Challenges for today

Prayer for today

Today, I am grateful for

"Then Jesus said to the disciples, 'Have faith in God.'"
Mark 11:22

DAY 18
MORE FAITH

Today's Date:

Read Matthew 17:1-20

F or three years, the disciples were privileged to spend their days traveling with Jesus. They listened to him teach. They were with him when he prayed. They watched him heal the sick. They were present for one miracle after another. Everything that Jesus did, they witnessed firsthand. However, when a desperate father came to them for help, they were powerless. Once again, I have to say that I can understand their dilemma. My earliest memories are of being in church. I can distinctly remember what I was wearing one Sunday, standing on a church pew at age 3, listening to the choir sing. I was so intent on seeing what was happening because my father was singing in the choir. Throughout my childhood, being in church on Sunday was an unspoken rule. We never missed church; when I had kids of my own, we never missed church either. Anytime the church doors opened, we were present. However, as we can see by the disciples' experience, being present is not enough. Faith cannot be acquired by just "being there".

When Jesus said, "Have faith in God" He was talking to them individually. Each one of them needed to acquire their own personal, living faith in God so that they would not be powerless if Jesus was not around. How can we each acquire our own personal, living faith in God? Jesus said that all we needed was a faith as small as a mustard seed, but where can we get it? When can we get it? We will need it because there will be a time when we find ourselves face to face with a crisis. We acquire and grow our mustard seed faith in the nitty-gritty of everyday life. Let your Big Idea be an opportunity to cultivate your mustard seed faith. Let the items on your Resource List become your prayer requests.

Write down your needs and concerns. Pray as if your life depends on it. Wait and watch what happens in the days to come. Keep your eyes open for opportunities. I know that as you observe, you will see the answers to your prayers unfold in unexpected ways. On top of it, as you look back on your prayer journal, you will notice that your faith has grown. The things that were so troubling to you in previous years will look smaller. You will feel much more confident in your relationship with God, your faith in God and your ability to pray in faith.

> *"Faith is the confidence that what we hope for will actually happen; it gives us assurance about things we cannot see." Hebrews 11:1*

DAY18 NOTES

Thoughts for today

Plans for today

Challenges for today

Prayer for today

Today, I am grateful for

"If you go as far as you can see, you will then see enough to go even farther." -John Wooden

"But when Daniel learned that the law had been signed, he went home and knelt down as usual in his upstairs room, with its windows open toward Jerusalem. He prayed three times a day, just as he had always done, giving thanks to his God." Daniel 6:10

DAY 19
PRAYER

Today's Date:

Read Daniel 6

D aniel was one of the most powerful men in Babylon and he was about to be thrown into the lion's den. When Daniel was a young man, he was taken as a captive by the Babylonians after they conquered Jerusalem. King Nebuchadnezzar ordered his troops to bring back trophies, including some of the most beautiful, intelligent young men from the royal families. The King wanted these young men to become his servants. Daniel never saw Jerusalem again. In the king's court, Daniel threw himself fully into the tasks he was given. In spite of the sorrow of captivity, he excelled in everything he did. He rose in the ranks. His reputation for excellence and trustworthiness grew. As the events in Daniel 6 were becoming more volatile, Daniel prayed. He never stopped praying.

Daniel's relationship with God was defined by prayer. His prayer routine was so well-known that his jealous, Babylonian co-workers used it to trap him. Three times each day, Daniel left work, went into his house and prayed. He consistently thanked God and pleaded with Him for the restoration of Jerusalem and his people. God responded to Daniel in many ways, sometimes through dreams and visions. The accounts of God's answers to Daniel's prayers are recorded in later chapters of the Book of Daniel. Daniel's commitment to prayer was so intense that he chose being thrown into the lion's den rather than go a day without prayer. A day without prayer would mean a day without communication with God. What is the role of prayer in your life?

> *"Asking is the beginning of receiving. Make sure you don't go to the ocean with a teaspoon." -Jim Rohn*

DAY 19 NOTES

Thoughts for today

Plans for today

Challenges for today

Prayer for today

Today, I am grateful for

"Pray in the Spirit at all times and on every occasion. Stay alert and be persistent in your prayers for all believers everywhere." Ephesians 6:18

"Don't you realize that in a race everyone runs, but only one person gets the prize? So run to win!" 1 Corinthians 9:24

DAY 20
SELF-DISCIPLINE

Today's Date:

Read 1 Corinthians 9:24-27

D aniel was a self-disciplined man. His self-discipline propelled him to the front of the class as a youth and to the highest leadership positions as an adult. From what we know about him, even when he became second in command to the king, he continued his daily routines. Our society today seems to place more value on celebrity and fame than on self-discipline. However, Daniel's life is a testimony to the power of self-discipline. You are 20 days into this 40-day journal. Have you settled into a daily rhythm with this book? Stop and look at your daily schedule. Is it aligned with the schedules you prepared a few days ago? Self-discipline is hard because the discipline is coming from within you. Don't get discouraged. Push!

As I am writing this, the 2012 London Olympics are taking place. I am mesmerized by the athletes and their dedication. I was speechless after watching double amputee Oscar Pistorius run the 400 meters. There is no doubt that Oscar has self-discipline. In your own life, approach your goals as if you were an Olympian preparing for an event. Approach your goals as if you were Daniel trying to excel in a foreign land. Your self-discipline to accomplish your goals will propel you forward.

"We all have dreams, but in order to make dreams come into reality, it takes an awful lot of determination, dedication, self-discipline and effort." -Jesse Owens

DAY 20 NOTES

Thoughts for today

Plans for today

Challenges for today

Prayer for today

Today, I am grateful for

"This is my command — be strong and courageous! Do not be afraid or discouraged. For the Lord your God is with you wherever you go." Joshua 1:9

DAY 21
COURAGE

Today's Date:

Read Mark 3:1-6

Jesus was courageous. He was not afraid to be himself or to act according to his convictions. Even in the face of opposition, Jesus remained authentic. Creating your vision, values and mission statements required you to be authentic. It took courage. Staying true to yourself, your plans and your convictions will require even more courage. "Politically correct" is a phrase heard often in our culture. Being politically correct involves not saying anything or doing anything that would offend anyone or contradict the prevailing cultural themes. One politically incorrect statement made in public and broadcasted through social media can end a career.

Jesus was not concerned about being politically correct. He had no intention of allowing the man with the withered hand to leave that synagogue without being healed. He knew what day it was and He knew that the religious leaders were watching him closely. Jesus chose to be authentic and to act according to His convictions. When He told the man to stretch out his hand, everyone could see that it had been healed. I don't know what you have written down in your plans. I don't know what God has called you to be and do. Whatever it is, continue to be authentic. Be courageous.

"Bravery is being the only one who knows you are afraid." -Franklin P. Jones

DAY 21 NOTES

Thoughts for today

Plans for today

Challenges for today

Prayer for today

Today, I am grateful for

"Heroism is endurance for one moment more."
-George F. Kennan

"Remember to observe the Sabbath day by keeping it holy. You have six days each week for your ordinary work, but the seventh day is a Sabbath day of rest dedicated to the Lord your God. On that day no one in your household may do any work..."
Exodus 20:8-10a

DAY 22
REST

Today's Date:

Read Exodus 20:8-11

God says in this passage that we have six days to do our regular work, but the seventh day is a Sabbath day of rest, dedicated to Him. Have you built a Sabbath day of rest into your schedule? Any type of rest is a struggle for me. Workaholism is a bad habit I've wrestled with for a long time. My choices of careers and work assignments haven't helped either. Success in project management and proposal writing favors the workaholic who will stop at nothing to get the job done, get it done first, and get it done best. For countless years I have worked relentlessly, even knowing what I know about the relationship between health and rest and more importantly, knowing what I know about the Sabbath rest. As a leader, I knew that I was not only modeling workaholism, but also I was expecting the same from my team members.

Why was that? I believed that more hours and more intensity would always result in a better outcome. Recently though, I was confronted with a project that defied the logic of more work = more output = better outcomes. I was frustrated, tired and out of ideas. In fact, I was so tired I couldn't even think, but then I got a "God idea". Get some rest! I thought, "Rest? Isn't that just for the sick?" Hmm… honestly, as many times as I have read these scriptures in Exodus 20, I just didn't think to apply them to my own life. What have I done about my bad habit? Well, I have built rest into my schedule now and not just bedtime rest. I have had to acknowledge that rest provides the mind, the body and the spirit with space to recharge, recover and revive. I decided to agree with God.

"Take rest; a field that has rested gives a bountiful crop." -Ovid

DAY 22 NOTES

Thoughts for today

Plans for today

Challenges for today

Prayer for today

Today, I am grateful for

"So there is a special rest still waiting for the people of God. For all who have entered into God's rest have rested from their labors, just as God did after creating the world." Hebrews 4:9-10

"Then the Lord turned to him and said, "Go with the strength you have, and rescue Israel from the Midianites. I am sending you!" Judges 6:14

DAY 23
ALONE

Today's Date:

Read Judges 6:1-16

The Midianites had descended on their nation, stripping them of their food and livestock; destroying their crops. Gideon's family was starving. In Judges 6, Gideon had been sent out alone to thresh wheat in a wine press. His family hoped that the Midianites would not detect him before he made it home with the grain. This passage tells us that instead of the Midianites, Gideon met the Angel of the Lord. This angel gave him another, more dangerous mission: defeat the Midianites – alone. Gideon vehemently rejected what the Angel had to say.

He believed he was the least capable person from the poorest family in Israel. He was convinced that he would not be able to accomplish that task. Maybe he had grown up being told that he was the least capable and least valuable. Maybe that's why they had sent him out to the wine press alone. Maybe his family had considered their options and decided that the need for grain outweighed the risk of losing Gideon.

What's your self-concept and how did you develop it? Do you have confidence in yourself or do you turn down new opportunities because you don't think you can do it? Gideon's self-concept was so low that he boldly told the Angel of the Lord that it was impossible for him to complete the request. However, notice that God already considered Gideon to be the person He had designed him to be: a mighty warrior. It didn't matter that he was hiding in the winepress. The capacity to complete the task was already inside Gideon. The same principle applies to us. God already considers you the person He designed you to be. You already possess the capacity to complete your mission. You, alone, have to decide to get up and get started.

> *"It's not who you are that holds you back, it's who you think you are not." -Unknown*

DAY 23 NOTES

Thoughts for today

Plans for today

Challenges for today

Prayer for today

Today, I am grateful for

"Jacob was terrified at the news. He divided his household, along with the flocks and herds and camels, into two groups." Genesis 32:7

DAY 24
FEAR

Today's Date:

Read Genesis 32

Jacob experienced fear. As he was fleeing from his father-in-law, Laban, he found himself running straight into the path of his brother, Esau. Both of these men had serious grudges against Jacob. To make matters worse, Jacob was not running alone. All of his wives and children, servants, herds and other earthly possessions were trapped between the two men who had a grudge against him. He spent that night alone – in fear. Fear of the future – fear about what may happen next – can grip us. An unexpected cancer diagnosis, the loss of a job, or any other situation that blindsides us can induce fear. Sometimes, we have created the situations that we fear. Jacob did. He set the events in this account in motion when he stole Esau's birthright (Genesis 27:2-10).

Regardless, the physical sensations associated with fear are universal. Shortness of breath, sweaty palms, racing heartbeat, feelings of doom and lack of appetite are just a few of the symptoms people experience when they are fearful. You may very well have experienced some these symptoms at one time or another. I have. These symptoms are our physical reaction to our circumstance. Fortunately, fear does not diminish God's presence or power in our lives. In fact, God's presence and power can become more tangible when we are in our bleakest moments. Jacob had his most powerful encounter with God when he was most fearful of the future. Embrace your fear. Know that God is close. Be assured that His promises to you are still secure.

"Everything we want is on the other side of fear."
-Farrah Gray

DAY 24 NOTES

Thoughts for today

Plans for today

Challenges for today

Prayer for today

Today, I am grateful for

"Give all your worries and cares to God, for he cares for you." 1 Peter 5:7

"This is what they sang: 'Give thanks to the Lord; his faithful love endures forever!'" 2 Chronicles 20:21b

DAY 25
PRAISE

Today's Date:

Read: 2 Chronicles 20:1-30

*I*n life, we can expect unexpected trouble. One morning, my husband went outside to walk our dog, Jack, like he did every morning at 6:30 a.m. Walking into the driveway, he noticed something very strange. My car was not there! Someone had silently stolen it in the middle of the night. We never would have expected that. Until that moment, our day had been going according to our routine. All was well. Until the moment when messengers came to King Jehoshaphat, he was probably enjoying the routines of a typical day. All was well in his kingdom. He never expected to find out that three armies were marching against him. He was terror-stricken. When you find yourself in the middle of an unexpected, troubling event, what is your first response?

My first response is usually nausea, spreading from my stomach to my throat. Goosebumps rise up on my arms and I want to shrink. In his fear, Jehoshaphat directed the people to fast and pray. He stood in front of the Temple and begged God to help them. He reminded God of His promises to Israel. God's response was that they should march into battle with their praise team leading the way. Circumstances began to change in their favor the moment they began to sing praises to God. Praise released God's power on their behalf. Likewise, when we are looking at a troubling situation and fear is rising up in us, we need to stop, go in the direction of the trouble and praise God. Praise is the evidence that we believe God is greater than the circumstances in front of us. He can and will help us. When we praise, God's power will be released on our behalf.

> *"Let everything that breathes sing praises to the Lord!"*
> *Psalm 150:6*

DAY 25 NOTES

Thoughts for today

Plans for today

Challenges for today

Prayer for today

Today, I am grateful for

"Let us strip off every weight that slows us down, especially the sin that so easily trips us up. And let us run with endurance the race God has set before us."
Hebrews 12:1b, 2

DAY 26
PASSION

Today's Date:

Read Hebrews 12:1-3

What are you willing to endure to realize the completion of your life mission? Are you willing to endure hardship, opposition or shame? Have you ever thought about it? The race set before Jesus was to culminate at the Cross. He knew that the time would come when He would have to face it. There was no way around it. Redemption and restoration waited on the other side of the Cross. In today's reading, we are told that Jesus endured many hardships, opposition and shame as he moved closer to the finish line. He never quit or gave up. He kept His mind focused on the end goal. His joy was the anticipation of this race being completed.

Likewise, we are encouraged to do the same. With Jesus as our ultimate role model of passion, we are encouraged not to grow weary or lose heart in pursuit of our goals. Rather than dread the hardships, we should redefine these things as our joy, knowing that we are moving closer to the completion of our earthly mission. Completing your goals will involve hard work and sacrifice; more than likely, it will involve some opposition and conflict as well. Unexpected problems or hardships may arise, testing your resolve. Allow Jesus to be your ultimate role model. If you are convinced that your mission is worthy, your joy will become the anticipation of its completion.

> *"Nothing of great value is ever accomplished by a reasonable person. Be unreasonable; the world is counting on you." -J. Sewell Perkins*

DAY 26 NOTES

Thoughts for today

Plans for today

Challenges for today

Prayer for today

Today, I am grateful for

"Decide that you want it more than you are afraid of it." -Bill Cosby

"Even when there was no reason for hope, Abraham kept hoping — believing that he would become the father of many nations. For God had said to him, 'That's how many descendants you will have!'" Romans 4:18

DAY 27
HOPE

Today's Date:

Read Romans 4:16-25

Hope is not subject to natural laws. It cannot be measured or captured on a timeline. However, having hope is a necessity for anyone with a big idea. Hope is a tangible lifeline; a cord stretching from the present moment to the moment hoped for. Abraham was a man who possessed hope. The promises that God made to him were long-term and futuristic. Abraham pressed forward in his everyday life, gripping the lifeline of hope, convinced that he was going to receive everything in those promises. Do you possess hope? Do you live your everyday life fully convinced about your own plans? Even more importantly, do you live your everyday life fully convinced that God is for you as much as He was for Abraham? These are important questions for you to answer.

In Abraham's life, God spelled out the big picture. He did not give Abraham the details. Every event in Abraham's life, on his way to obtain the promises, was not pleasant. There would be dark days that would make most people give up hope. This passage of scripture says that even when there was no logical reason for hope, Abraham maintained hope in God. He hung on. As you develop and write out your plans, there will be unexpected events you could not have planned for. Some of them will not be pleasant. Some of them will threaten to throw you off course, but let Abraham be your role model for hope. Never let go of the lifeline.

> *"Once you choose hope, anything's possible."*
> *-Christopher Reeve*

DAY 27 NOTES

Thoughts for today

Plans for today

Challenges for today

Prayer for today

Today, I am grateful for

"Keep a green tree in your heart and perhaps a singing bird will come." -Unknown

"Then he went on alone into the wilderness, traveling all day. He sat down under a solitary broom tree and prayed that he might die. 'I have had enough, LORD,' he said. 'Take my life, for I am no better than my ancestors who have already died.'"

1 Kings 19:4

DAY 28
AGAIN

Today's Date:

Read I Kings 19

*E*lijah wanted to die, but he kept running. He felt that he had done everything that God had asked him to do. He had prophesied faithfully. Miraculous signs had been performed through him. The bitter drought had ended exactly when Elijah said it would and his reward was that he was now being pursued by Queen Jezebel, who wanted to murder him.

Elijah was exasperated, exhausted, famished and frightened. Why had God allowed this to happen to him? Living had lost its meaning. In a modern day adaptation of this story, the writers would most likely describe Elijah as clinically depressed and suicidal, overcome by his circumstances. Forty days later, Elijah found himself in a cave on Mount Sinai, the mountain of God. This is the same mountain that Moses spent 40 days on and then descended with the Ten Commandments.

This mountain was sacred. God's presence was known to dwell there. What would God have to say to him? Did God care? We read that God indeed met Elijah there. God wanted to know why the prophet of Israel was cowering in a cave in Egypt. God told him to go back to Israel, to the place he had been fleeing. God told Elijah to go back to the situation he feared. Along the way back, God would provide men to assist him complete his mission. God did have something to say to Elijah; God did care. Most importantly, God let Elijah know that his depression did not signify the end of his mission. Instead, it was just an interlude before he was to begin again. Don't get discouraged on your journey. You may just need to take a break, like Elijah did. Allow God to prepare you to begin again.

"Don't give up trying to do what you really want to do. Where there is love and inspiration, you can't go wrong." -Ella Fitzgerald

DAY 28 NOTES

Thoughts for today

Plans for today

Challenges for today

Prayer for today

Today, I am grateful for

"At times our own light goes out and is rekindled by a spark from another person. Each of us has cause to think with deep gratitude of those who have lighted the flame within us." -Albert Schweitzer

"And Jonathan made a solemn pact with David, because he loved him as he loved himself. Jonathan sealed the pact by taking off his robe and giving it to David, together with his tunic, sword, bow and belt." I Samuel 18:3-4

DAY 29
FRIENDS

Today's Date:

Read 1 Samuel 18:1-4, 1 Samuel 20:1-17

I believe that good friends are strategically placed in our lives by God. A good friend is a blessing. A good friend will encourage you, make you laugh and tell you the truth. A good friend will go beyond the extra mile to help you. In his life, David had one close friend and confidant, Jonathan. David would not have survived long enough to be king had it not been for Jonathan. In my life, I have been blessed with some good friends. They do encourage me, make me laugh and tell me the truth, even when I don't want to hear it. They have gone the extra mile for me on many occasions. Where would I be today if not for these good friends?

I have never had a spear thrown at me, but I have been through some tough times. My good friends helped me get through them. What role do friends play in your life? In David and Jonathan's case, their friendship became intertwined with their respective life goals and legacies. Jonathan helped David escape death and become king. Jonathan's legacy lived on because David provided for his sole surviving son and his family. Make time in your schedule to cultivate your key friendships. Be a good friend. Recognize and appreciate your roles in each other's lives. There may come a moment when you know that you were placed strategically in each other's lives, just like David and Jonathan.

> *"Every man should keep a fair-sized cemetery in which to bury the faults of his friends."* -Henry Ward Beecher

DAY 29 NOTES

Thoughts for today

Plans for today

Challenges for today

Prayer for today

Today, I am grateful for

"A true friend is someone who thinks that you are a good egg even though he knows that you are slightly cracked." -Bernard Meltzer

"Saul now urged his servants and his son Jonathan to assassinate David. But Jonathan, because of his strong affection for David, told him what his father was planning. 'Tomorrow morning,' he warned him, 'you must find a hiding place out in the fields.'" I Samuel 19:1-2

DAY 30
ENEMIES

Today's Date:

Read I Samuel 19:1-10

*E*nemies can materialize in your life when you least expect it from the most unlikely places. The most damaging enemy is the one who you had once counted as an ally. Usually, that person knows you so intimately that they know how to strike an effective blow. These are not just physical blows, like Saul attempted when he threw a spear at David. Friends-turned-enemies or "frenemies" can damage you at the core of your being, leaving you unbalanced and feeling a little suspicious of everyone. In David's case, Saul became a life-long "frenemy" of David's. Saul's irrational jealousy and bitterness toward David never subsided. Saul pursued David and made David's life difficult until the day Saul died in battle.

I think David had the right idea though. Don't hang around trying to figure out why that person is behaving as an enemy. Remove yourself. Hopefully, there are no spears involved! Is there an enemy in your life right now – a family member, former friend, co-worker, or boss? Don't let your enemy distract you such that you lose track of yourself and your mission. Pray that God would help you to forgive this person. Never take an opportunity to damage that person in return. Forgive. Move on. In time, God will sort out the situation for you.

"Faithless is he that says farewell when the road darkens." -J.R.R. Tolkien

DAY 30 NOTES

Thoughts for today

Plans for today

Challenges for today

Prayer for today

Today, I am grateful for

"So she turned to Abraham and demanded, 'Get rid of that slave woman and her son. He is not going to share the inheritance with my son, Isaac. I won't have it!'" Genesis 21:10

DAY 31
CHALLENGES

Today's Date:

Read Genesis 21:1-21

On many occasions, Abraham exhibited tremendous faith in God. He is noted in the Bible as one of the greatest examples of faith. Romans 4:21-22 tells us that because of Abraham's faith, God considered him righteous. However, Abraham was not exempt from the challenges of everyday life. One challenge that he knew very well was family conflict. In today's reading, Abraham is confronted with the conflict between the mothers of his two sons, Sarah and Hagar.

The conflict had become so bitter that Sarah demanded Hagar and her son be thrown out of the family. Abraham knew that being separated from the safety and resources of the family meant death for Hagar and Ishmael, but Abraham also knew that Sarah did not care.

This family conflict threatened the one thing Abraham had wanted for so long: children. However, rather than abandon his faith for what he desired, Abraham chose to obey God again. Walking through this challenge molded his character and strengthened his faith. Have you noticed that people of great character and the strongest faith are often the ones that have faced the greatest challenges? What does this say to you and me? I think that it says we should be encouraged to embrace our challenges. My dad used to say that I should thank the people who caused me the most conflict. Instead of being frustrated with them, I should say, "Thank you for making me wiser and stronger!" Today, embrace your challenges. Like Abraham, trust God and His Word for what to do. You are getting wiser and stronger.

"Nothing is an obstacle unless you say it is." -Wally Amos

DAY 31 NOTES

Thoughts for today

Plans for today

Challenges for today

Prayer for today

Today, I am grateful for

"I am not afraid of storms, for I am learning to sail my ship." -Louisa May Alcott

"If you follow this advice, and if God commands you to do so, then you will be able to endure the pressures, and all these people will go home in peace." Exodus 18:23

DAY 32
WISDOM

Today's Date:

Read Exodus 18

Moses was overwhelmed in his leadership position. After leading the people of Israel out of Egypt, he remained their key decision maker in daily matters. He was also their intermediary with God. Day in and day out, he stayed busy troubleshooting the problems of the nation. People lined up, hoping to talk to him about their dilemmas. He was so busy that did not have any time for his family. He had even sent his wife and their two sons home to live at her father's house.

One day, his father-in-law came to visit. Jethro was thrilled to hear about all the good things that were happening, but he was shocked when he witnessed how Moses was handling his leadership role.

Jethro also knew that Moses was ignoring his role as husband and father. Moses' wisdom was highly sought after, but he did not possess the wisdom to troubleshoot the problems in his own life. We all need a Jethro. We all need a mentor who can look at, listen to and assess what we are doing professionally and personally. Like Moses, we may become so immersed in what we are doing that we become blind to what we are doing. A mentor represents wisdom. If you are willing to receive it, a mentor's wisdom will move you beyond your blind spots to a higher level of leadership in all areas of your life. Is it time for you to seek out a mentor?

> *"Impart as much as you can of your spiritual being to those who are on the road with you and accept as something precious what comes back to you from them."*
> *-Albert Schweitzer*

DAY 32 NOTES

Thoughts for today

Plans for today

Challenges for today

Prayer for today

Today, I am grateful for

"All great achievements require time." -Maya Angelou

"David and his men tore their clothes in sorrow when they heard the news. They mourned and wept and fasted all day for Saul and his son Jonathan, and for the Lord's army and the nation of Israel, because they had died by the sword that day." 2 Samuel 1:11-12

DAY 33
GRIEF

Today's Date:
Read: 2 Samuel 1

D ictionary.com defines grief as "keen mental suffering or distress over affliction or loss". Since nobody is immune to suffering, nobody is immune to grief. At some point in our lives, grief will visit us. My father's death triggered my profound grief. I did not tear my clothing, like David did, but I lost my appetite for a very long time. When I did eat, the food seemed to have no flavor. I had trouble sleeping. I stopped writing in my journal. Nothing seemed to interest me anymore. My father had been my sounding board and one of my biggest fans. Now, his voice was silent. From reading this passage of scripture, I can sympathize with David's grief.

Jonathan had been his best friend and confidant. Their friendship had spanned a major portion of David's life. The callous young man who brought the news of Jonathan's death most likely expected a reward. However, David's profound grief had unleashed not only anguish, but anger. In our life goals, we never think to create space for grief. However, when it comes, grief can expand and crowd out our most carefully crafted plans. Have you had an event occur in your life that triggered grief? What emotions did you experience? How did you move through it? Be encouraged. Allow yourself to grieve. Grieving is never easy, but over time, the anguish of grief will fade.

"We must embrace pain and burn it as fuel for our journey." -Kenji Miyazawa

"My vision is blurred by grief; my eyes are worn out because of all my enemies." Psalm 6:7

DAY 33 NOTES

Thoughts for today

Plans for today

Challenges for today

Prayer for today

Today, I am grateful for

"He is a wise man who does not grieve for the things which he has not, but rejoices for those which he has."
-Epictetus

"Praise the Lord! How joyful are those who fear the Lord, and delight in obeying His commands." Psalm 112:1

DAY 34
JOY

Today's Date:

Read Psalm 112

Psalm 112 is one that I have recited out loud many times. I read it out loud as a prophetic declaration over my life. I declared that I was joyful as I feared the Lord and obeyed his commands. My children would be successful everywhere and light would shine in the darkness for me. Every verse in this psalm speaks to my life and what I desire. Today, read Psalm 112 out loud. Listen to the words as you speak them. Speak them with conviction. Allow joy to rise in your heart; joy that these verses are coming to pass, right now.

What? You say you are too logical for that? I have news for you: God's reality encompasses more than what we can understand in our earthly life. Remember, at the moment God called Gideon a mighty warrior, he had not yet seen even one battle. God called Abraham the father of many nations before he had any children at all. I believe this psalm was included in the Bible for you and me. This psalm declares to us the outcomes of a life of obedience and dedication to God. Encourage yourself. Be joyful!

> *"Your success and happiness are in you. Resolve to keep happy and your joy and you shall form an invincible host against difficulty." -Helen Keller*

"The Lord is my strength and my shield. I trust him with all my heart. He helps me, and my heart is filled with joy. I burst out in songs of thanksgiving."
Psalm 28:7

DAY 34 NOTES

Thoughts for today

Plans for today

Challenges for today

Prayer for today

Today, I am grateful for

"Perhaps the Lord will help us, for nothing can hinder the Lord. He can win a battle whether he has many warriors or only a few!" 1 Samuel 14:6b

DAY 35
DANGER

Today's Date:

Read 1 Samuel 14:1-23

I love heroes. I love stories and books about heroes. I love movies about heroes. My favorite book and movie trilogy of all time is *The Lord of the Rings*. Why do I love heroes so much? Heroes take on tasks that are so big and so filled with danger, yet they never give up. Just when you think all is lost, they win. The dangerous situation is thwarted. Jonathan was such a hero. While his father and his closest advisors sat under a pomegranate tree, Jonathan was devising a plan to defeat the Philistines. The odds were against Israel. They

Thrive!

were outnumbered by the heavily armed and well-resourced Philistines. However, Jonathan told his armor bearer, "The Lord can win a battle whether he has many warriors or a few." Jonathan's faith in God outweighed the faith of his nation's leaders.

When Jonathan and his armor bearer climbed over the mountain and down into the Philistines' camp, God met them there, sending a panic throughout the Philistine army. He sent an earthquake. That day, the Philistine army was defeated. Jonathan did not have any extraordinary, supernatural powers. He was a man with faith in God. He saw a problem and believed that God would show up and help him solve the problem. His faith affected the course of history in his nation. He was the hero of that story. Be the hero of your own story. Allow your faith to grow and outweigh what others might believe. Just like in Jonathan's case, the Lord will meet you where you are. He will show up. You will win.

"Nothing will ever be attempted if all possible objections must first be overcome." -Samuel Johnson

178

DAY 35 NOTES

Thoughts for today

Plans for today

Challenges for today

Prayer for today

Today, I am grateful for

"Smooth seas do not make skillful sailors." -African Proverb

"The Lord will work out his plans for my life — for your faithful love, O Lord, endures forever. Don't abandon me, for you made me." Psalm 138:8

DAY 36
FAILURE

Today's Date:

Read Psalm 138

This psalm is an encouragement. David wrote this psalm of praise and thanksgiving to God in the midst of his troubles, when he was surrounded by enemies. David praised God for His unfailing love and faithfulness. He was confident that God would give him strength and save him. He was also confident that God's plans for his life would succeed, regardless of how bleak the situation looked. Have you ever faced failure? David is our example when it comes to failing. He failed morally when he murdered Uriah so that he could commit adultery with Bathsheba.

He failed as a father when he gave no response after his daughter Tamar's rape. He nearly failed as a king when his son Absalom attempted to overthrow his reign. David experienced failure. However, he never abandoned his faith in God. He never drifted away from honoring and praising God. He acknowledged his failings and his troubles, but in spite of them he also trusted God to see him through. Here's the truth that David discovered: God will never fail. He will always fulfill his promises. He always answers our prayers and provides us with strength to endure. Our failures do not impact God's character or His activities. Praise God!

"Just when the caterpillar thought the world was over, it became a butterfly." -Unknown

"Your next step beyond failure could be your biggest success in life." -Debbie Allen

DAY 36 NOTES

Thoughts for today

Plans for today

Challenges for today

Prayer for today

Today, I am grateful for

"Remember that failure is an event, not a person." -Zig Ziglar

"This is the message you have heard from the beginning: we should love one another." I John 3:11

DAY 37
LOVE

Today's Date:

Read I John 3:11-24

*L*ove is a foundational character trait that John the Apostle wrote about in his letters. A leader loves. A leader loves those whom he or she serves with an unconditional, sacrificial love. A leader is willing to sacrifice for the best interests of those he or she serves. John knew firsthand about the loving, sacrificial leadership modeled by Jesus. On the opposite end of the spectrum, there is nothing more devastating or discouraging than serving alongside a narcissistic leader. The focus of this person's plan is love of self. This leader will readily demand sacrifice from others, take credit for work done by others and will manipulate for self-promotion.

Tread lightly. As you move through your life and leadership opportunities arise, check yourself against John's words in this chapter. Yes, we want our plans to be successful, but are we in any way misusing our power or expecting more of others than ourselves to bring our plans to fruition? Do our plans have a residual benefit for anyone other than ourselves? Have we considered how we might be an asset to our community in whatever we do? I have heard it said many times: love is a verb. Our love is evident through our actions, not our words or good intentions.

> *"Dear children, let's not merely say that we love each other; let us show the truth by our actions." 1 John 3:18*

"All you need is love. But a little chocolate now and then doesn't hurt." -Charles M. Schulz

DAY 37 NOTES

Thoughts for today

Plans for today

Challenges for today

Prayer for today

Today, I am grateful for

"Long ago the Lord said to Israel: 'I have loved you, my people, with an everlasting love. With unfailing love I have drawn you to myself.'" Jeremiah 31:3

"But thank God! He has made us his captives and continues to lead us along in Christ's triumphal procession." 2 Corinthians 2:14a

DAY 38
MILESTONES

Today's Date:

Read John 16

In May 2012, my daughter, Vanessa took the Medical College Admission Test (MCAT). She had just completed her junior year of college and would spend her summer preparing medical school applications. The most important thing in her mind, at the time, was getting accepted into medical school during her senior year. However, I reminded her that getting accepted into medical school was just the beginning of another stage of her journey. If she wasn't careful, she would miss the opportunity to reflect on and celebrate her achievements. The "here and now" was what needed to be recognized. Vanessa had worked diligently through three years of college and had prepared herself to complete the MCAT. This was an achievement worthy of recognition and celebration. She had persevered and endured. When she came out of the testing center, we drove to a restaurant of her choice to celebrate.

We celebrated completing an intermediate step on her journey to become a doctor. The next stage of her journey was going to be more arduous. It is easy to miss the opportunity to recognize and celebrate completed intermediate goals. Sometimes, we are looking so far ahead into the future that we don't see the good work that has been accomplished. We anticipate the hard work that is still ahead, brushing off what we have completed with diligence, hard work and endurance. Often the completion of a particular intermediate goal is the key to completing the entire project. If my daughter had not prepared to take the MCAT, her goal of becoming a doctor could never be realized. You cannot enter any medical school without submitting your MCAT scores. Take time out to celebrate your accomplishments. Consider them to be milestones on your journey. Say to yourself: "I am moving forward. I am moving closer to my ultimate goal. Congratulations!"

"Do not pray for an easy life, pray for the strength to endure a difficult one." -Bruce Lee

DAY 38 NOTES

Thoughts for today

Plans for today

Challenges for today

Prayer for today

Today, I am grateful for

"The principal thing in this world is to keep one's soul aloft." -Gustave Flaubert

"Anyone who believes in me may come and drink! For the Scriptures declare, 'Rivers of living water will flow from his heart.'" John 7:38

DAY 39
STRENGTH

Today's Date:

Read John 7:37-39

I started writing this book during the 2012 Presidential Election campaign season. Candidates and elected officials at every level have been bombarding the airwaves with what they will do in the next political term, if elected or re-elected. I am thankful for those who are willing to take on the challenges of government, but their ability to keep their promises is subject to many factors that are outside of their control. *God is never going out of office.* His ability to keep His promises doesn't ebb and flow with circumstances. It remains unchanged because ultimately, circumstances are subject to Him. One of His promises is this: whoever believes in Jesus, rivers of living water will flow from their core being. "Rivers of living water" is a powerful metaphor in scripture.

Rivers are mentioned in both Revelation 22: 1-2 and Ezekiel 47:1-12. Both of these rivers are described as flowing from the throne of God, stimulating life, healing and abundance. The potency of this water remains constant because the source is God's throne. This is the river flowing from you and me as we place our faith and hope in Jesus. Whatever we do and wherever we go, this river is flowing, stimulating growth, healing and abundance all around us. Don't think I am overstating the power of this promise. As we are mindful of this promise, the outcomes of our efforts can't help but be successful. The strength we exert to make it happen will have been powered by this never-ending, consistently potent, river of life flowing from the throne of God. This river is the source from which we will **thrive**!

> *"You must do the thing which you think you cannot do." -Eleanor Roosevelt*

DAY 39 NOTES

Thoughts for today

Plans for today

Challenges for today

Prayer for today

Today, I am grateful for

"Be thankful for what you have; you'll end up having more. If you concentrate on what you don't have, you will never, ever have enough." -Oprah Winfrey

"I will praise the LORD, and may everyone on earth bless his holy name forever and ever." Psalm 145:21

DAY 40
GRATITUDE

Today's Date:

Read Psalm 145:1-21

Today is the last day of this interactive journal. Take time today to review your experiences over the last 40 days, both the successes and the challenges. Consider what you have learned about yourself, about your life and about God. What will your next steps be? Also, take time to thank God for what has happened in your life through this journal. If you were to write a psalm of praise to God, what would it say?

My Psalm of Praise:

_____

_____

_____

_____

_____

_____

_____

_____

_____

_____

"Gratitude is the fairest blossom which springs from the soul." -Henry Ward Beecher

DAY 40 NOTES

Successes

Challenges

What did you learn about yourself?

What are your next steps?

Your prayer

"An attitude of gratitude brings opportunities."

-Unknown

"If you would lift me, you must be on higher ground."
-Ralph Waldo Emerson

FURTHER READING

Bender, Susan, "Everyday Sacred"

Bolles, Richard N., "What Color is Your Parachute? 2013"

Bolte Taylor, Jill, "My Stroke of Insight"

Brizendine, Louann, "The Female Brain"

Brizendine, Louann, "The Male Brain"

Brzezinski, Mika, "All Things at Once"

Cloud, PhD, Henry, "Necessary Endings"

Covey, Stephen, "Seven Habits of Highly Effective People"

Duhigg, Charles, "The Power of Habit"

Gordon, Jon, "Seed"

Jones, Laurie Beth, "The Path"

Moore, Beth, "Believing God"

Tharp, Twyla, "The Creative Habit"

Ueland, Brenda, "If You Want to Write"

"If you can't see the bright side of life, buff up the dull side." -Unknown

"Dear friend, I hope all is well with you and that you are as healthy in body as you are strong in spirit." 3 John 1:2

ABOUT THE AUTHOR

Rev. Linda Pulley Freeman is an associate pastor at Trinity Church in Miami, Florida and the Executive Director of its Peacemaker Family Center. With more than 26 years of program management experience, as both an environmental engineer and a social service director, she leads this "one-of-a-kind" faith-based community outreach ministry with excellence and energy. An ordained minister, a member of Leadership Florida and a Fellow at the Georgetown University Center for Juvenile Justice Reform, Linda obtained a M.S. in Environmental Engineering from Stanford University and a B.S. in Chemical Engineering from the University of Michigan. Linda has been married to her husband, David, for 27 years. They have four children in their lives: Zachary and his wife, Daniella, Vanessa, and Nina, their niece.

"The way a long work is completed is by daily tapping the imaginative impulse. That's got to be so strong that it never dies in the course of the whole performance."
-Paul Horgan

CPSIA information can be obtained
at www.ICGtesting.com
Printed in the USA
FFOW03n0936290117
31755FF